Don't Unpack Your Bag Here: Becoming Unstuck and Moving Forward
ISBN: 978-1-7373229-0-0
LOC ID: 2021910849

Copyright © Tamika Flores

Publisher, Editor and Book Design: Fiery Beacon Publishing House, LLC
Fiery Beacon Consulting and Publishing Group

Graphics: FBPH Graphics Team, Dashona Smith

This work was produced in Greensboro, North Carolina, United States of America. All rights reserved under International Copyright Law. No portion of this publication may be reproduced, stored in any electronic system, or transmitted in any form or by any means (electronic, mechanical, photocopy, recording or otherwise) without written permission from the Tamika Flores. Brief quotations may be used in literary reviews. Unless otherwise noted, all scripture references have been presented from the New King James version or Amplified version of the bible. All definitions in this work have been presented by Google Dictionary (copyright)

DON'T UNPACK YOUR BAG HERE!

Becoming Unstuck and Moving Forward

By:

Tamika Flores

TABLE OF CONTENTS
Thank You's
Introduction
Salvation Prayer

Chapter 1: Why is Deliverance Important?	9
Chapter 2: Holy Spirit	17
Chapter 3: Don't Let the Dust Settle	23
Chapter 4: Condemnation vs Conviction	29
Chapter 5: Call a Plumber-My Pipes Broke!	33
Chapter 6: Don't Unpack Your Bags Here!	39
Chapter 7: Power in Abiding in Him	47
Chapter 8: What are You Filling Your House Up With?	53
Chapter 9: Stop Wasting Your Oil!	57
Chapter 10: I WILL NOT GO BACK!	61
Connect with the Author	65

THANK YOU'S

I want to thank my Lord and Savior Jesus Christ! I could not had done this without His Grace and Mercy!

Special thanks you, to my Amazing Husband, Andre Flores, who supporting me throughout this entire process. Love you!

My awesome children, Andre, Amir, Anthony, Ahmad, Tamia

My beautiful grandchildren, Zoey, Taylor and Connor

My mother has her own special place, her guidance, prayer, correction and most of all the push! Love you!

Bishop Barbara Glanton, thank you for your foundational teachings of prayer, love and keeping our hearts right. Thank you for all your prayers not only for me but for my family.

Pastor Craig Pickett and First Lady Pickett, I thank you for your love, support and wisdom. To the entire Breakthrough Ministry Family, I love and appreciate you!

Pastor Bryan and Jackie Lowe of Freedom Ministries Church and Outreach Center, your unwavering love, support and giving us the freedom to be TPOM will be forever sketched in our hearts!

Thank you to everyone that has prayed, encouraged and pushed me! I love you! It has not gone unnoticed.

SPECIAL RECOGNITION

True Purpose Outreach Ministry, words cannot express the love we have each of you. You all have literally weathered many storms with us, and we are forever grateful! Thank you for all your prayers, countless sacrifices, and hearts of generosity.

We are a special unique ministry and God's hand is upon us! Love y'all!

This is our Winning Season!

THE INTRODUCTION

Wow is all I can say right now! This has been a serious journey for me and an amazing eye opener, too. Each chapter the Holy Spirit downloaded, contains very practical but powerful messages that I hope transform your life. I pray that you will begin to burn with an unquenchable fire to seek the Lord like never before. <u>Don't Unpack Your Bags Here</u> speaks to those seasons in our lives when we feel paralyzed, not motivated, disinterested, as if we are backsliding into a dark mindset, and so much more. The devil wants to stop our progress in anything that we do that will bring glory to God. This book and the message it carry is a movement! I believe a harvest of souls are going to be drawn to Jesus and they will become free from torment from the enemy. Over the last twenty-one years of my walk with God, it has not been easy and many times I just wanted to give up BUT GOD! Proverbs 24:16 (TPT) says this,

For the lovers of God may suffer adversity and stumbles seven times, but they will continue to rise over and over again. But the unrighteous are brought down by just one calamity and will never be able to rise again.

I hope and pray that everyone that reads this book will become inspired to dig deeper and live again, smile again, laugh again and re-imagine again. I know we have heard this before, but we have to trust the process and GROW through the process. You know when you subscribe to certain clothing sites that require a monthly fee for you to purchase an outfit or shoes and if you decide not to shop that particular month it gives you the option to skip a month? Well, in our walk with Christ we cannot skip - if we do, we can miss so much. It is not that simple, and I personally do not want anything if it has to come so easy. I desire more - to gain the wisdom and understanding of the journey the Lord has given me. Keep moving forward! Keep pushing!

SALVATION PRAYER

If you have never accepted Jesus as your personal Lord and Savior, say this prayer with me:

Father forgive me for all my sins.

Come into my heart, live in me and help me to live for you.

Father I believe that your Son Jesus, died, but you rose Him up from the grave.

Father I accept your Son Jesus as my personal Lord and Savior, to serve Him all the days of my life!
In Jesus' name,
Amen

If you said this prayer, the angels in heaven are rejoicing! Welcome to the family. Your life will never be the same!

CHAPTER 1
Why is Deliverance Important?

He brought me up also out of an horrible pit, out of the miry clay, and set my feet upon rock, and established my goings.
Psalm 40: 2 (TPT)

When we hear the word *deliverance* what is the first thought that come to your mind? Can I be honest with you? The thought that come to my mind is,

"Yes, I know deliverance is important, but how do I stay delivered from whatever that thing is, or situation that God is delivering me from?"

Deliverance is part of our Christian walk and the only way to understand it is to study the Word of God, pray and ask the Holy Spirit to give us understanding. I can understand that deliverance can look different to some people depending on the type of ministry you attend or attended. I believe deliverance has to be taught in a way that the person on the receiving end understands how important this is in their lives. I remember the first deliverance service I went to; it was at the church where I accepted Jesus Christ as my personal Lord and Savior. I remember there were plastic bags, boxes of tissues and garbage cans. This was a true deliverance service led by Evangelist White and the Lord use this woman of God in such a mighty way that night.

Let's define the word *deliverance*. Deliverance means, "to be rescued, to be set free and to release." I want to describe deliverance in way of "release". In order to understand release, you first have to understand what it is you need to be released from. *Luke 4:14 AMP says,*

"The Spirit of the Lord is upon me (the Messiah), Because He Has Anointed Me to preach the Good News to the poor. He Has sent Me to Announce <u>Release</u> (pardon, forgiveness) To the Captives, and recovery of sight to the blind, to set free those who are oppressed (downtrodden, bruised, crushed by tragedy).

Over the years I have heard the words "deliverance" and "set free" almost at the same time whether hearing it preached, taught or written. I have found myself stuck at the *release* part of deliverance. I knew that I had been forgiven and that God sent Jesus to let us know we have been released from the bondage of sin, but to forgive myself for my shortcomings, mistakes, disobedience, or not completing a task seemed incomprehensible. This place can cause you to be stuck and leave you no longer progressing. Romans 8:1 AMP tells us,

Therefore, there is now no condemnation [no guilty verdict, no punishment] for those who are in Christ Jesus [who believe in Him as personal Lord and Savior].

We will discuss condemnation in Chapter 4.

When we accept Jesus as our personal Lord and Savior, we are no longer in chains, but instead **RELEASED**! Our sins have been forgiven! So, if you make mistakes or fall short to the glory of God, repent, release it and KEEP IT PUSHING! Do not stay there in that mindset that you are not good enough and that you are always making mistakes. Learn from it by getting to the root to why it happened! Take it to God in prayer and be a student to the HOLY SPIRIT by gleaning from His teachings. We will discuss the Holy Spirit in chapter 2.

So, I know many of us either have a deliverance ministry or have been raised in one or both. Deliverance is so much more than laying of the hands and casting out devils. Yes, that is a vital part, but to understand why Jesus was sent to set the captives free, release, preach the gospel is just as vital. Deliverance has many different parts and casting out devils should not be the only part we learn or teach. I will state again, it is a vital part but not the only part.

I have been blessed to have come from two amazing deliverance ministries where I have been in many prayer lines and deliverance services. I find when you leave those services there has to be an ongoing work so you can understand what took place in your life. I call it the "tune up phase." Some of us need a tune up, just like when you take your car for a tune up; the mechanic normally makes you aware what needs changing and what will need changing soon. Allow the Holy Spirit to give you a tune up. Ask the Holy Spirit to search your heart and mind daily.

Search me, O God, and know my heart; Try me, and know my anxieties.

Psalms 139:23 NKJV

I have made so many mistakes by not focusing on the signs that was before me. God will give us indicators to allow us to take a closer look at that shift in our moods, sudden feeling of heaviness, depression and the list goes on. We have to closely examine where we are to see exactly what is going on. You may ask "how do we examine the indicators?" We do this by, prayer, fasting, studying God's Word and speaking to a mature Christian that God has led you to share your experiences with. Therapy is another way to examine some areas in our lives that we have not dived into. I am so grateful for the Lord opening my heart to go to therapy. It has changed my life, but one thing I must push is that you have to do the work that is given to you. I know when I had my first session, I did not realize how much I had suppressed. I want to share something with you - I choose to go to a Christian therapist who flows by the Holy Spirit. I know there are some dynamic people in this field, but I think we have to be led by God as to who He has assigned to us during this sensitive season in our lives.

How do we release the power within us?

As I ponder on this question that was given to me earlier today, I want to add what the Lord downloaded into my spirit about the words "detached" and "attached." I believe there are many ways power can be release within us, but we have to be detached from the place that has us in bondage. Let's us first look at the word "detach"; it means:

"to separate especially from a larger mass and usually without violence or damage."

We can also include the word disengage which means:
"to release from something that engages or involves."

You might ask, "okay where are you going with all of this?" Well, we must ask the Holy Spirit to reveal to us! What is in our lives that we must be released from? Is it a bad relationship, unforgiveness, bitterness, anger, or any form of sin that goes against God's Word? The most important part of this process is how it attached itself to you. The word "attach" means:

> *"to bring (oneself) into an association, to bind by personal ties (as of affection or sympathy)."*

I know most of us have heard "don't open the door to Satan" before. To elaborate a little further, I am reminded of the scripture *Romans 12:2 (TPT),*

> ***Stop imitating the ideals and opinions of the culture around you but be inwardly transformed by the Holy Spirit through a total reformation of how you think. This will empower you to discern Gods will as you live a beautiful life, satisfying and perfect in his eyes.***

CHAPTER 2
Holy Spirit

"But when the Helper (Comforter, Advocate, Intercessor-Counselor, Strengthener, Standby) comes, whom I will send to you from my Father, that is the Spirit of Truth who comes from the Father, He will testify and bear witness about ME.
John 15:26 (AMP)

There is no way I can discuss the content of this book without speaking on the greatest teacher of all which is Holy Spirit. I know there are hundreds of books about this subject, and I encourage you to read and study concerning this. I am going to share what I have learned throughout the years about the Holy Spirit which changed my life and still is changing my life to this day.

Many years ago, I was at a church service in Patterson, New Jersey, and this awesome woman of God from New Orleans was teaching about the Holy Spirit. This was the first time I had heard the Greek word for Holy Spirit (Paraclete) explained and the definition given was

"one called alongside to help." Wow! Not only does the Holy Spirit live inside of us as believers of Jesus, but the Holy Spirit walks alongside of us. I have heard countless teachings on the Holy Spirit, but at this moment, it was like so personal to me! Holy Spirit walks alongside me, yes me! I am the one that cannot get right in certain areas in her life and yet God can use a woman like me, yes ME!

Jesus spoke of the role of the Holy Spirit in *John 14: 16-26 AMP*. I love the way the Amplified Version lists Holy Spirit roles, and the first role was "helper." We can see in the Greek definition of the Holy Spirit; it states, "He walks alongside to help us." The other roles listed are "Comforter, Advocate, Intercessor-Counselor, Strengthener and Standby." The Word of God said in *Deuteronomy 31:8*, "He will never leave us nor forsake us," and He surely holds true to His Word!

Holy Spirit reveals all truths. He is more than a feeling or energy, and once we beginning to understand His role in our lives, we will begin to understand the power that dwells on the inside of us as a believer. Paul speaks of this in *2 Corinthians 12:9* where Jesus told him "My Grace is sufficient for you." Here is the most important part to me of this verse - the word "sufficient." We first must understand that we are insufficient without Jesus but through God's Grace and the working of the Holy Spirit we are strengthened through Him.

We need the Holy Spirit even when it comes to prayer. Ephesians 6:18 speaks on always praying in the Spirit and on every occasion. The other important part of Holy Spirit is that He is a revealer of all truths and very consistent with the testimony of the nature of Jesus. Everything we need to know about Jesus, Holy Spirit will show us and teach us. (*John 16:13 NKJV*) Holy Spirit will bring everything back to your remembrance and when you do not know what to say, He will form your words for you. (*John 14:26 NKJV*.) When I speak at job interviews, at churches, in front of stone-faced people or give presentations and get very nervous, I begin to pray,

Holy Spirit speak through me!
Form my words and take over!

We have the greatest companion that lives inside of us and walks alongside us. It is so much to cover when it comes to the Holy Spirit, but I pray this is a start of your journey to discover and seek the power that dwells in you as a believer of Jesus Christ.

Scriptures on the Holy Spirit

John 14:26

Ephesians 1:13; 4:30; 5:19

Jude 1:20

Romans 6: 3

Romans 8:26-27

Titus 3:5

John 3: 5-8

1 Thessalonians 1:6

2 Corinthians 13-14

Romans 15:13

Galatians 5:16-19

There are so many more scriptures that you can continue to dive into. My desire in sharing the above references with you, is that you will search the Word of God on your own and allow the Holy Spirit to open your heart and mind to understand His flow and to understand His role in your life as a believer of Jesus Christ. I encourage you to read each scripture in a different translation so you can have a broader understanding of the Word of God, find a commentary that you are comfortable with, and realize that we must invest in getting tools for growth in our Christian walk. Bible plans are good, but they are not enough if used alone. Using these resources should cause me to dive into that topic more or search the scripture out that is attached to that plan deeper. Now do not get me wrong, bible plans have opened my heart and mind to countless of lessons but do not depend on that being your only source of study.

CHAPTER 3
Don't Let the Dust Settle!

But he answered me, "My grace is always more than enough for you, and my power finds its full expression through your weakness." So, I will celebrate my weaknesses, for when I'm weak I sense more deeply the mighty power of Christ living in me.
                    2 Corinthians 12:9 (TPT)

When dust settles on an object, you cannot clearly see what the original state of that object was before the dust settled on it. The word "settle" means to:

"**migrate to and organize (an area, territory, etc.); colonize.**"

Dust comes from a various of things like hair, clothing fiber, bacteria, dust mites, bits of dead bugs and so much more. I know this is gross right? Trust me, I am going somewhere with this. When dust settles on a thing it takes up territory; how long is determined by how long we take to dust it off.

Now what has God told us to do but we allowed the dust or cares of this world to settle on it? Remember dust comes from various things, so the dust-off rejection! Dust off unforgiveness! Dust off comparison! Dust off lack! Dust off failure! Dust off condemnation! Has it settled on your dreams and visions that God has spoken to you? It is time for you to dust it OFF and bring it back to its original state of clarity. Dust off procrastination and finish the book, school, business plan, and everything else God has placed in your hearts to do! If you are anything like me, I have so many journals that are incomplete and there are many guaranteed streams of income in those journals. So many of us feel that,

"I know God has more for me than a 9 to 5! I know I am supposed to have my own business, my own school! I know that I was created to become blessing to many."

Yes, dust it off with obedience, consistency, trust and faith to know God with equip you to complete the vision before you! It is time that you become a human duster through your obedience, praise and worship that will blow the dust right off! I know many of us like to spring clean! We begin to dust off areas that we have not done in a while and just like that, space is bright and sometimes the air is even clearer. I am reminded of the scripture *Isaiah 42: 9,*

"Behold, the former things have come to pass, And new things I declare; Before they spring forth I tell you of them."

One thing that we must understand is that the devil does not want us to progress, and he will stop our progression any way he can. We must submit to God; the Word of God says resist the devil and he shall flee from us. (*James 4:7)* The latter part of this scripture is quoted more than the first part, because in some areas in our lives, it is hard to submit completely to God if we can be honest with ourselves and with God.

Submitting to God is our power over the enemy.

When we dust off the areas in our lives, clarity is given, or clarity is being restored back to its original state. Do not let the dust settle any longer on your purpose that God has pre-destine for you even before you were in your mother's womb, He has a plan for you. (*Ephesians 1:11*) God always accomplishes every purpose and plan in His heart.

    Many of you may think that it is too late to accomplish some dreams and goals in your life but how would you know that if you do not dust it off? I pray this chapter encourages many of you to go back and revisit that amazing plan; to go back to school, start the business, open the school, write the book and many more amazing plans that God has place in your life to do. I had to decide that I was no longer going to allow the dust to settle on me becoming an author. I had to realize that this was so much bigger than me and God desires to use me to reach His people and share in His love and Gospel of Jesus Christ - that is His plan, and it shall be accomplished.

Use this space to write things down that need to be dusted off your life!

CHAPTER 4
Condemnation vs. Conviction

There is therefore now no condemnation to those who are in Christ Jesus, who do not walk according to the flesh, but according to the Spirit.
Romans 8:1 (NKJV)

Condemnation is a beast, and in this chapter, I am going to be very open and honest with you regarding my own experience with condemnation for many years. Let's first define the word *condemnation.*

[1]*"an accusation, or a scolding or punishment for a bad act."*

Condemnation feeds off of a person that does not fully understand the love of God (Agape) has for them. Let's take a moment to dive into the meaning of condemnation. The first word is "**accusation**", and we know who accuses

---

[1] *yourdictionary.com*

us before God - yes Satan! (*Revelation 12:10 NKJV*) The next word is "**scolding**" which means "harsh reproof." The Word of God says the Lord disciplines those whom He loves. (Proverb 3:12) The Lord also said in His Word to repent!

So they went out and preached that men should repent [that is, think differently, recognize sin, turn away from it and live changed lives].

Mark 6:12 AMP

So just imagine someone who is experiencing condemnation. They are going through accusations, scolding, believing that God is mad at them or that He does not love them because they failed. This is an example of torment, and I lived this way for years while being born again, filled with Holy Spirit and very active in ministry. Condemnation is like Velcro - it sticks onto anything that is contrary to what God says in His Word. Its sticks to your wounds from childhood to adulthood, insecurities, offenses, unforgiveness, rejection and the list unfortunately can go on. When condemnation is not addressed, the enemy Satan will send a spirit of ISOLATION and then they have a TURN UP TORMENT PARTY! Do not give the devil place in your life!

Now the way I look at conviction is like a nudge to let you know sin was committed and we need to repent. Conviction is defined as, **"a feeling of responsibility or remorse for some offense, crime, wrong, etc., whether real or imagined."** God is not going to condemn us, and we must understand we have to be alerted when we have fallen short. Conviction can be looked at as an alert system that the Holy Spirit uses to give us a heads up that we did something that went against God's Word or character. Look, we all fall short of the glory of God, (Romans 3:23) but the most important part is the getting back up and continuing to move towards God! Do not allow the devil to keep you down. I know many of you might wonder, "will God love me the same way He did before I failed?" The answer is, **YES** child of God. Nothing can separate us from the love of God (Romans 8: 38-39).

We must fully understand the love that God has for us, and when we do the lies of Satan will fall to the ground and will not be able to attach itself to our minds and hearts. God's love will destroy every lie you believe about yourself. Here are some examples of lies that come from the enemy:

I am always messing up.

Here I go again doing the same thing yet again.

I am not good enough.

I am not smart enough.

It's too late for me to start over.

These are just handful of what we speak over our lives. So, I want you to take a moment and think about the lies that you have been speaking over your life. I heard this many years ago, "your words form the world around you." If your life is full of murmuring and complaining, guess what, there will be no peace.

Let's look at it another way, your words can either attract God presence or the enemy and you can choose the words you speak! We blame the devil for the environment we created because of the words that come out of our mouths. I am not telling you not to express yourself or talk about how you feel. Do not stay in the place like the title of this book! Don't unpack your bags there! Keep going! Speak life over yourself and your situation!

CHAPTER 5
Call a Plumber-My Pipes Broke!

Search me [thoroughly], O God, and know my heart; Test me and know my anxious thoughts; And see if there is any wicked or hurtful way in me, And lead me in the everlasting way.
Psalms 139: 23-24 (AMP)

    This title came in my spirit when thinking about how, when we leave things in our lives unchecked and do not properly heal from hurt, loss, rejection, abandonment and betrayal, it clogs up our spiritual pipes. Where we once were able to flow in certain areas in our lives with ease it becomes frustrating and stressful. This leads us to a place where we must ask ourselves what is in the way from us moving on and pushing forward.

    Why are plumbing and plumbers needed? Plumbing is as important to your residential or commercial building as oxygen is to the body. Wow, I love this statement, and it is very true! When do we decide to call a plumber? When the sink, toilet, etc. is no longer operable. It is also stated that our plumbing system should be checked every few months to make sure it is maintaining its functions properly. Now let's look at our spiritual life - we must maintain our spiritual walk daily, renew our minds, examine our hearts, and deal with things that come up that disrupts our plans and uncertainties. We must realize that if we do not keep a daily check, we can have a clog that will back up and overflow into our marriages, families, jobs, and relationships. Everyone knows that plumbing is expensive, and when left unchecked, can cost a person a ton. So, we can look at this in our own spiritual walk. It can cost us so much and especially TIME! Can I share with you the amount of time I lost because I did not want to deal with the clogged areas in my life and the damage that was done due to not dealing with it? Things that I was holding on to and was afraid to release literally had my life clogged up.

When I was looking up the definition of *clog* the word **"hinderance"** came up, but the best way to define a clog is, "a blockage or something that is getting in the way". We must really ask the Lord to constantly search our hearts and mind daily to prevent a spiritual clog.

What are some of the signs that you are spiritually clogged?

- Unforgiveness
- Bitterness
- Fear (Anxiety)
- Holding grudges (remember grudges holds you not the other person)
- Rejection
- Abandonment
- Feeling stuck
- Worry, doubt and unbelief
- Depression
- Procrastination

When you begin to see these things that are clogging your spirit, ask the Lord to help you and trust the process. Becoming spiritually unclogged from the things that hinder us from going forward takes time and work on our part. You can do this with Gods help and being sensitive to the Holy Spirit's prompting.

List some areas in your life that need to be unclogged!

_____

_____

_____

_____

_____

_____

_____

_____

_____

_____

_____

_____

_____

_____

_____

_____

CHAPTER 6
Don't Unpack Your Bags Here!

When a demon is cast out of a person, it goes to wander in a waterless realm, searching for rest. But finding no place to rest, it says, 'I will go back and reoccupy the body I left.' When it returns, it finds the person like a house swept clean and made tidy, but empty.

Luke 11: 24-25 (TPT)

I really wanted to explain further in this chapter what *'Don't Unpack Your Pack Bags* Here' means. I know most people do not like the process of moving, but when you unpack the boxes and everything in your home or office is coming together you look around and say to yourself it was worth it. Well, there is a flip side to this. Sometimes we unpack our bags, get comfortable and remain in places that are not ordained by God. We unpack unforgiveness, anger, bitterness, comparison, fear, hurt, rejection and then we begin to dwell there. The longer we stay the worst it gets and then we begin to invite others. When we invite others, especially if they are unpacking the same issue, we tend to stay in these places longer. Let me give you an example - if two or more people you meet unpack church hurt and no one in that group has healed from this, you end up with a three-bedroom apartment full of hurt people. We all have heard the saying "hurt people hurt people." Until one of these people get healed from what they have unpacked and bring the process of healing back to the group (everyone process is different) it will only get worse. Now you can also unpack your bags alone and the enemy will use everything in his power to make you feel stuck, alone, paralyzed, shameful, and full of failure, but God can also bring healing and deliverance in your life through Christ.

    The Lord gave me such an amazing revelation for Luke 11: 24-26 (TPT). When an unclean spirit leaves a person, Jesus says that it goes through dry places seeking rest and when it finds none it revisits the house/body from which it came and when it returns it finds the house swept and put into order. Here we can unpack in these clean rooms, praise and worship, prayer, boldness, the Word of God, and faith. Jesus said the rooms were swept and put into order, yet the rooms were empty, and this is very important remember from chapter one. We talked about deliverance and there is more to deliverance than casting out devils; there is spiritual maintenance that must take place as well. Let me say this, when we fill our body/house with the things of God, the enemy will not have access to what he had access to previously. You will be able to discern even when the enemy has made his way in your neighborhood. You will begin to pray, declare, and decree and let that devil know that he has no permission to enter back in your body/house. You cannot even afford to allow that joker at your doorstep and some of us need to get rid of the key under the mat! Yes, we have things we have not totally surrendered to God - let it go! We cannot give the devil any place in our lives!

God loves us unconditionally and He wants us to know who we are in Him. Listen there are some things in our lives that has happened to us that require, professional help (pray for a spirit-filled believer) in the field of therapy that can help you, along with reading the Word of God, and praying. Far too long especially in the Black community we have shunned professional help like counseling, but praise God over the last several years that has changed, and more people have shared their testimonies and the stigma is slowly leaving regarding counseling. Many celebrities have used their platforms to share the importance of mental help, and yes, we have a long way to go but I do see the progress. I recently decided to go to therapy because I needed some help in processing somethings in my life that had surfaced back up in the form of some deep insecurities and it has changed my life completely. We must decide to do the work and trust the process.

Do not unpack your bags and remain in a space where you are not growing; your peace is being sucked out of you slowly, and your past is at your doorstep. In Luke 11: 24-26 (TPT), Jesus talks about when the enemy comes back to where he previously once lived at that joker brings seven times more evil spirits worse than the first ones. So, let us examine the space that we are in right now and if peace is absent from it then you need to examine what is going on in your life. Trust me we must do this daily because the enemy wants to stop our progress. We must also examine the relationships that we have in our lives both past and present. I have heard this for many years, there are some people that come in our lives only for a season, but we tend to let them stay longer not realizing that their time has expired. This does not mean they are bad people, but God's ways are not our ways, and we must continuously trust His plan. What I am saying is this - don't unpack your bags in those relationship that were meant to be a season and you unpacked for several seasons.

Listen, I understand that many of us including myself do not like change, but I had to understand change is vital. Yes, change is also meant to break up patterns in our lives that will cause us not to grow! A great example of a pattern that needs to be broken is not completing what we have started, and believe or not, it can be passed down to our children as a learned behavior. I noticed this in one of my children - they will complete a task when pressure is applied but the danger of this type of pressure is that you cannot operate in your full potential when pressure shows up. The devil likes it when we rush to complete or rush to get to a place, because he is then free to invite his cousins anxiety, frustration and aggravation. I was literally in my car several years ago studying for an exam and then went to class to take the test; that is so not healthy or good but, in my mind, I passed the test. Despite "passing" the question remained - did I retain information, or did I just memorized it to get done with the exam? I believe we miss so many amazing opportunities when we do not plan well or when we work under pressure. Planning is a huge part of our purpose; I am learning this at this moment, but if we do not, myself included, prepare in the areas of our purpose, we will not experience the fullness of what God wants to do through us.

    Okay, let me give you example about me. I know God has called me to the educational field but I had to trust God to open a door for me to return to school so He could prepare me for what He had in store for me in this field. If you know God has called you to be an entrepreneur then start preparing by gathering information about the type of business you are looking to open, google similar businesses in your area, read articles, books, take up training classes or YouTube or whatever it takes to prepare. Most importantly, seek God through prayer and fasting in all that you do and TRUST THE PROCESS.

List three areas in your life that you have to pack up and move!

_____

_____

_____

CHAPTER 7
Power in Aiding in Him

> You are already clean because of the word which I have spoken to you. Abide in Me, and I in you. As the branch cannot bear fruit of itself, unless it abides in the vine, neither can you, unless you abide in Me. I am the Vine, you are the branches. He who abides in Me, and I in him, bears much fruit; for without Me you can do nothing.
>
> John 15: 13-15 (NKJV)

When I need to be reminded about how important my relationship with Jesus is, I will read John 15. We need complete dependence and constant connection, and the branch depends on the vine. This text is so broad and covers a lot, but one word that stuck out to me over the years and that word is **abide**. I remember when I first read the meaning of abide; it stated, **"to dwell, remain"** but today I have realized there is another side to abide. We must CHOOSE to abide in Him, and this can be challenging at times, but God will give us the strength and strategy to do it.

Spending time with the Lord is so important, and the enemy knows this; that is why for most of us it becomes a battle. Now let's first talk about what spending time with the Lord looks like. I know with being a wife, mother, and Pastor, it can become extremely difficult to find that intimate time with God especially if you are working on top of all the other countless things that go on throughout the day, so you must find time during the day to spend time with the Lord. I choose the mornings because it is a great way to start my day, and everyone is still asleep. What people do with their time with the Lord can be different; some will play worship music, pray, or read the Word of God. My personal advice is first set the time. Sometimes the times can also change; the Lord might start getting you up at various times, and the rest will follow. I do believe it is vital that we study the Word of God and pray. We must choose daily to seek Him and the more we do this the more we grow in Him. Let me tell you I have struggled with this for years because I began to see my time with the Lord like routine, but it is so much more than a routine. We should embrace our time with the Lord with excitement but sometimes let's be real, we have to push ourselves. It is time to be honest, we do not always come in His presence with excitement. We have seasons in our life when it is extremely hard to due to circumstances like loss, betrayal and rejection. I was always taught that this is the time you draw to God and not away from Him. There has been plenty of times in my life where all I had was a "Lord, I thank You" because I was going through so much at the time but that was my prayer. Our hearts are what the Lord looks at. The posture of our hearts is what matters, not how many words you can pray and how many books of the bible you can read in an hour. This is what I mean by routine - we check off things like "okay, I read this today. I prayed this long", but did that time you spent with the Lord change you? You know, I had to understand that sitting quiet is also spending time with the Lord and listening for instructions. Just being in the stillness of the Lord is amazing, and it takes time to understand that. Sometimes God wants us to be quiet. I suggest that you have a notebook ready and pen because you will never know what He will begin to download in your spirit.

    The more I realize, knowing who I am in Christ my prayer life is growing, not so much in minutes and hours but by ***faith and trust in God***. When you begin to learn who God, Jesus and the Holy Spirit is, you will begin to see and understand prayer and reading the Word of God on another level. I will also encourage you to study the Word and not just read it; you will get such an amazing understanding and Holy Spirit to help you to open your understanding and to give you clarity as to what God's Word is saying to you.

Write down a few points you learned about ABIDE!

CHAPTER 8

What are You Filling Your House Up With?

And my God will liberally supply (fill until full) your every need according to His riches in glory in Christ Jesus.
Philippians 4:19 (AMP)

When we think of remodeling our home or buying new furniture, we should be excited! We begin to look at different designs and some of us will even go as far as watching DIY shows to give you different ideas for the space you are designing. Here is the thing I observe within in myself - I can go hard on many things and be so super detailed but why can't I do the same when it comes to my spiritual walk? I should be just as detailed as I am with anything else in my life.

We should be so mindful as to what we fill our spiritual houses up with and be as detailed as possible. Let's look at our minds like it is our front yard; we should not let anything enter our front door that is not of God.

Casting down imaginations, and every high thing that exalted itself against the knowledge of God and bringing into captivity every thought to the obedience of Christ;

2 Corinthians 10: 5 (KJV)

Our minds are the entry way that we have to renew daily. Now once we enter into the front door, we have to fill the rooms up with prayer, the Word of God, praise and worship, a heart of thanksgiving and gratitude. Do not give the devil any place or space in your house.

Neither give place to the devil.

Ephesians 4:27(KJV)

There are certain rooms in the houses that are seen but the contents in these rooms are hidden like an attic or a basement. These are the rooms that hold our insecurities, our hurts, our imperfections; these are things we do not want anyone to see. What is the purpose for the attic in our homes? Attics are the space between the roof and the ceiling of the highest floor of the house. Attics are easy to overlook. Attics are sometimes dark and trips to the attic are sometimes rare, but attics are big deals in your home because it brings comfort and energy efficiency in your homes. We have to make sure we take care of those things that seem hidden but are great value in our lives. Like our past, we tend to allow the enemy to bring shame to us, but our past will fuel our purpose. Even rooms in our homes serves a purpose. When we do not use rooms in our homes, what normally happens to them? They become cluttered with items that we toss, and we deem those items not usable. I can just imagine how many ideas, inventions, books, curriculum's and so much more that was thrown into a room in our minds and hearts that we deem unusable.

Let's look at the basement; the original purpose of it was for storage space for water, wine, and food. Being underground spaces, they were traditionally damp, musty places wherein whatever is stored should be protected in glass or tin. I believe there are some things that God allows to be protected in our lives regarding dreams and visions that cannot be release until His perfect timing.

He who dwells in the shelter of the Most High will remain secure and rest in the shadow of the Almighty [whose power no enemy can withstand].

Psalms 91:1 (AMP)

God's timing is the perfect timing and God's will is perfect. What I really want to bring out in this chapter is the importance of filling our spiritual house where the Lord dwells with His Word, praise, worship, gratitude, thanksgiving, and so much more. Do not give the devil access to your house!

CHAPTER 9
Stop Wasting Your Oil

There is precious treasure and oil in the house of the wise [who prepare for the future], But a short-sighted and foolish man swallows it up and wastes it.
Proverbs 21:20 (AMP)

When I first heard this said to me "Stop wasting your oil" at the time I felt like,

"WOW how can I waste my oil? I don't understand."

Here is the understanding that the Lord has given to me. Especially as a leader, we are constantly pouring into people daily. There are some people that you meet that are not ready to change or should I say submit fully to God, and sometimes we will mistake this as an assignment from God. You are constantly pouring your time, love, knowledge, wisdom, and nothing is changing within them. Now I know many would read this and say God plants the seed, someone waters it and God will bring the increase. See we must discern rightly regarding who we are to pour into; we are not junior Holy Spirit, and we do not need to handle and figure out everything in someone else's life because that is God's job. We must constantly ask,

"God, is this your will for me to be in this person's life ministering to them in this season?"

Our motives have, to be discerned rightly; we prematurely call seasons in our lives spiritual warfare and it can be a consequence of inviting a situation that God did not ordain at all. We are depleted, tired, drained, and not understanding what is going on in our own lives. In our reaction, we go back and re-examine the people, places and things that are in our lives.

Are they GOD ORDIANED OR FLESH FALSE DESIRES?

All good desires come from God! I know I have not always and may still miss God in this, but I have learned to ask Holy Spirit, "Is this your will for this person or situation to be in my life," and I will begin to see God moving or God will remove that person or situation from me. We must take the signs that the Holy Spirit will began to show us and move quickly.

I am a firm believer that we as leaders and non-leaders alike should flow from our overflow not our barely enough or halfway enough. Overflow to me means that we should be in a John 15 mindset, CONSTANTLY abiding in the Lord and dwelling with Him. Most of the time we will try to push through the half empty flow, and we will always crash. I just recently noticed that I tend to take on things, people and projects that sound like a great idea but is it a GOD IDEA for my life in this season? So, I must get in a habitual habit of asking the Holy Spirit for guidance and wisdom for every decision both big and small. This is also important - at first you may not see that situation as that big of a deal but a small out of order request can turn into a huge problem. I have made so many mistakes in not discerning. That small request can have a huge impact on my marriage, family and ministry. Don't be anxious for nothing!

Don't be pulled in different directions or worried about a thing. Be saturated in prayer throughout each day,

offering your faith-filled requests before God with overflowing gratitude. Tell him every detail of your life.
            -Philippians 4:6 (TPT)

I truly believe most of us do not believe that God wants to talk to us and have us tell Him about every detail of our lives. We tend to give Him the most important thing pertaining to our lives and leave out the small things. Is it that we do not believe? God is concerned about ALL of us, every detail both big and small. We have to be very conscience! Our time is very important, and we have to use wisdom on what to do with it.

Making the very most of your time [on earth, recognizing and taking advantage of each opportunity and using it with wisdom and diligence], because the days are [filled with] evil.
            Ephesians 5: 16 (AMP)

DON'T WASTE YOUR OIL!

CHAPTER 10
I WILL NOT GO BACK!

For the ones who restores the sinning believer back to God from the error of his way, gives back to his soul life from the dead, and covers over countless sins by their demonstration of love!
James 5:20 (TPT)

There is a level of determination that we have to possess regarding not wanting to go back to what God has brought us out of, and we have to take by force anything that gets in our way.

And from the days of John the Baptist until now the kingdom of heaven suffers violence, and the violent take it by force.

Matthew 11:12 (NKJV)

When I began the journey of writing this book, I wondered why God was not leading me to start with my memoir, but He had another plan and, trust, it is coming soon. When God uses me to speak, or teach He uses 99.9% of the experiences and trials from my life to be transparent to His people and 1% is from other people's experiences or what I have heard or seen.

I have been through so much - hardship, sexual abuse, low self-esteem, poverty, life as a teenage mother and a high school drop-out too, BUT GOD! I accepted Jesus Christ as my personal Lord and Savior when I was twenty-four years old, and it was the best decision of my life. I experienced condemnation for years as a believer but now I know that I had to FULLY understand that God loves me no matter what, flaws and all. God's love for us is unmatched to anything in this world!

O taste and see that the Lord [our God] is good; How blessed [fortunate, prosperous, and favored by God] is the man who takes refuge in Him.

Psalms 34: 8 (AMP)

We must begin to embrace the process and I know many have heard this so many times "It's a process", but it is a necessary journey that has to happen in our lives. The process is not easy and at times can be very painful BUT every part of it, God can and will use. We have to decide

EVERY day that we will not go back to where God has brought us from.

- I will not go back to depression!
- I will not go back to lack!
- I will not go back living in condemnation!
- I will not go back to low self-esteem!
- I will not go back to bitterness!
- I will not go back to that pity party!
- I will not go back to self-sabotage!
- I will not go back to comparison!

I truly believe we all have our "I will not go back" declarations and we have to decree them over our lives and our family's lives as well. I love the definition of pursue which means, **"to follow in order to overtake, capture, kill or defeat."** When we are following after Jesus, pursuing Him, we should not be passive because the enemy is not passive with us. We have to overtake every lie the devil is speaking to us and capture every assignment the enemy will try to throw at us. Do not stop moving, keep moving forward, keep progressing into everything God has called you to do.

Connect with the Author
Tamika Flores

Pastor Tamika Flores was born and raised in East Orange, New Jersey. She is all about her family. Tamika gave her heart to Christ in July 1998 and her life has never been the same.

Her foundation in ministry was and always will be prayer. She served as lay leader of the Intercessory Prayer Ministry, Usher, Altar Worker, and so much more. She was ordained as Elder and that is when she began to see God's hand on her life for ministry. In April 2014, when she was ordained as a Reverend on the same weekend, her and the family moved to North Carolina. God moved yet again on her life when she was ordained as a Pastor in December 2019.

She has been married for nineteen years to her best friend Andre Flores; they met thirty years ago! They are parents to five beautiful children and are grandparents to four grandchildren. They serve as founding leaders of **True Purpose Outreach Ministries** in Salisbury, North Carolina. Pastor Tamika is currently enrolled at Liberty University and will receive her BSW in Social Work.

Pastor Tamika has a heart for God's people and as a midwife she, with the help of the Holy Spirit, will push you to your purpose.

www.ingramcontent.com/pod-product-compliance
Lightning Source LLC
Chambersburg PA
CBHW070655050426
42451CB00008B/367